I Can Make Friends

Written by Chemise Taylor

Illustrated by Alexis B. Taylor

ISBN: 978-1-951573-67-6

www.myskillsbooks.com

Hello! My name is

George.

What is your name?

_____

- - - - - - - - - - - - - - - - - - -

_____

Hi! I'm Mike.

I am 10 years old.

How old are you?

2 3 8 4 11 7 12 9 6 5 14 13 10

Hey There! I'm Brian.

I live in Dallas, Texas.

Where do you live?

Hey! I'm Kevin.

I am in the 5ᵗʰ grade.

What grade are you in?

Hi There! I'm Lionel.

I like the color blue.

What is your favorite color?

Hello! I'm Donald.

I have 2 sisters.

How many brothers or sisters do you have?

Howdy! I'm Jessie.

I have a pet dog.

Do you have any pets?

Hey! I'm Sam.

I love cheese pizza.

What is your favorite food?

Hi! My name is Ben.

I love milkshakes.

What is your favorite drink?

Hey There! I'm Rickie.

I really like chocolate.

What kind of candy do you like to eat?

Hey! I'm Joshua.

I love to read books.

What is your favorite book?

Hi! They call me Skip.

I like Netflix shows.

What shows do you like to watch?

Hi! My name is Frank.

I love summertime.

What is your favorite time of the year?

Hey! Call me Jimmy.

I like to draw pictures.

What do you do for fun?

Hi! My name is Tim.

I love Christmas.

What is your favorite holiday?

Hi! Call me Henry.

I like monster trucks.

What toys do you like to play with?

Hey There! I'm Chris.

I like going to parks.

Where do you
like to go
and have fun?

Hi! Call me David.

I love lions and bears.

What is your favorite animal?

Hi! If I was a superhero,

I'd be Bill the Invisible.

What superpower would you like to have?

It was nice to meet you and I hope we can talk again.

I really like making new friends.

Book Details

Story Word Count: 305

Key Words: Friend, What, Hello, Hey, I'm, Love, Like, Have

Comprehension Check

- Name 2 types of greetings?
- Name 3 people from the story?
- Give at least one detail about 3 people from the story?

Reading Award

I CAN MAKE FRIENDS

This certificate goes to:

_____

for reading "I Can Make Friends"

Good Job!

www.ingramcontent.com/pod-product-compliance
Lightning Source LLC
Chambersburg PA
CBRC091141030426
42335CB00010B/210